Wee Sing®

Children's songs and fingerplays

by
Pamela Conn Beall
and
Susan Hagen Nipp

Illustrated by
Nancy Spence Klein

PRICE STERN SLOAN
Los Angeles

To our forgetful friends...

(and to our special wee ones, Hilary and Sean, Ryan and Devin)

Published by Price Stern Sloan, Inc.
11150 Olympic Boulevard, Suite 650
Los Angeles, California 90064

ISBN:0-8431-0606-X

36 35 34 33

PREFACE

How many times have you wanted to sing a song to your child and found you couldn't remember the words? This has happened to us so many times that we decided to compile a book of our favorite songs and fingerplays to share with our forgetful friends and their wee ones.

Music can create a special closeness and joy to those who experience it together. However, for a child, there is more to music than mere enjoyment. Language development, muscular coordination, body awareness, rhythmic proficiency, auditory discrimination and self confidence are a few of the benefits acquired from an early exposure to music. The young child is eager for musical and rhythmic experiences, thus providing a perfect time to introduce songs and fingerplays.

Music can also provide a positive resource for approaching those crisis situations with children. As the hour of waiting in the doctor's office is drawing to a critical climax, nimble those fingers, begin "Three Little Monkeys" and feel the knot in your stomach untie. Or, as the road sign reads 20 more miles, bellow out "a chick, chick here" and watch the scowl on Dad's face disappear as he joins in with "a chick, chick there." Music may be the answer in moving from crisis to calm.

We want to thank our many friends who have contributed to this book. For them, and for you, we hope *Wee Sing* will bring many special, enjoyable times with your wee ones.

Pam Beall
Susan Nipp

TABLE OF CONTENTS

Preface 3
Table of Contents 4

Waiter, just one more cracker, please.

Eentsy Weentsy Spider 8
Mother's Knives and Forks* 9
Here is the Beehive* 9
Clap Your Hands* 10
Grandma's Glasses* 10
Hickory, Dickory Dock 11
Three Little Monkeys* 12
Two Little Blackbirds* 12
Knock, Knock* 13
Little Green Frog 13
Jack and Jill* 14
Bumblebee* 15
Where is Thumbkin? 15
'Round the Garden* 16
Here is the Church* 16
Five Little Fishies* 17

How many more miles did you say?

This Old Man 19
Little Peter Rabbit 20
The Finger Band 21
Down by the Station 21
The Train 22
Bingo 23
John Jacob Jingleheimer Schmidt 24
Little Cabin in the Wood 25
Old MacDonald Had a Farm 26

*Titles with asterisks are fingerplays which are rhymes illustrated by the use of finger motions.

Another day, another diaper.

Good Morning 28
What Are You Wearing? 28
One, Two, Buckle My Shoe 29
Rickety, Tickety* 29
My Name and Address 29
The Alphabet Song 30
Right Hand, Left Hand* 30
Ten Little Fingers 31
Days of the Week 31
Rain, Rain, Go Away 32
There is Thunder 32
It's Raining 32
Twinkle, Twinkle, Little Star 33
'Round the Clock 33

Wiggleworm workout

Looby Loo 35
Now Tall, Now Small 36
Animal Poem* 36
Walking, Walking 37
Jimmy Crack Corn 37
Baby Bird 38
Ring Around the Rosy 39
Pop! Goes the Weasel 39
I'm a Little Teapot 40
I'm a Little Snowman 41
The Mulberry Bush 41
If You're Happy 42
Peter Hammers 43
Reach for the Sky 43
Three Blue Pigeons 44
One Elephant Went Out to Play 45
Head and Shoulders 46
Jack and Jill 46
This is the Way 47
Trot to Boston 47
Teddy Bear 48

Whew! It's bedtime.

Good Night 50
Sleep, Baby, Sleep 51
All Night, All Day 51
All the Pretty Little Horses 52
Hush, Little Baby 53

Another holiday...so soon?

Jack-O-Lantern* 55
Chickamy, Chickamy, Craney Crow 55
Ten Little Witches 56
Gobble, Gobble* 56
Over the River 57
Christmas is Coming 58
The Chimney* 59
We Wish You a Merry Christmas 59
Skidamarink 60

Index 61

Waiter, just one more cracker, please!
Today's Menu

EENTSY WEENTSY SPIDER

Actions:

a) make circles out of thumbs and forefingers, put tips together, twist upward b) wiggle fingers while moving downward c) push outward d) make big circle with arms over head e) hands in front, palms up, move up in rhythm

MOTHER'S KNIVES AND FORKS

(Fingerplay)

These are Mother's knives and forks,
(fingers interlaced, tips up)

This is Mother's table,
(flatten hands and arms)

This is Mother's looking glass,
(palms toward face)

And this is baby's cradle.
(palms up, rock arms)

HERE IS THE BEEHIVE

(Fingerplay)

Here is the beehive, where are the bees?
(fist with thumb enclosed to make hive)

Hidden away where nobody sees.
(place other hand over the hive)

Watch and you'll see them come out of the hive,
(closely watch hive)

One, two, three, four, five.
(very slowly, beginning with thumb,
fingers come out of hive one by one)

Bzzzzzzz......
(all fly away)

CLAP YOUR HANDS
(Fingerplay)

1. Clap, clap, clap your hands
   As slowly as you can.
   Clap, clap, clap your hands
   As quickly as you can.
2. Shake....
3. Roll....
4. Rub....
5. Wiggle your fingers....
6. Pound your fists....

GRANDMA'S GLASSES
(Fingerplay)

Here are Grandma's glasses,
(fingers around eyes)

Here is Grandma's hat,
(hands on head)

This is the way she folds her hands,
(fold hands)

And lays them in her lap.
(folded hands in lap)

Here are Grandpa's glasses,
(larger glasses)

Here is Grandpa's hat,
(larger hat)

This is the way he folds his arms,
(fold arms across chest)

Just like that.
(with emphasis)

HICKORY, DICKORY DOCK

2. [a] Hickory, dickory dock,
   The [b] mouse ran up the clock,
   The [c] clock struck two, (clap, clap)
   The mouse said, [e] "Boo!"
   [a] Hickory, dickory dock.
3. . . . The clock struck three, (clap, clap, clap)
   The mouse said,[f] "Whee!" . . .
4. . . . The clock struck four, (clap, clap, clap, clap)
   The mouse said,[g] "No more!" . . .

Actions:
a) hands in praying position, rock them left to right
b) wiggle fingers upward c) clap hands above head
d) wiggle fingers downward e) hands around mouth
f) hands up in surprise g) shake head no

THREE LITTLE MONKEYS
(Fingerplay)

Three little monkeys jumping on the bed,
  (tap three fingers on palm of opposite hand)

One fell off and bumped his head.
  (one finger falls off, then hold head)

Mama called the doctor and the doctor said:
  (hold phone by ear, dial in air)

"No more little monkeys jumping on that bed."
  (shake finger)

Suggestion: Repeat with "Two little monkeys..."
"One little monkey..."

TWO LITTLE BLACKBIRDS
(Fingerplay)

Two little blackbirds
Sitting on a hill,
  (pointer fingers up)

One named Jack
  (one hand forward)

And one named Jill.
  (other hand forward)

Fly away, Jack.
  (one hand behind back)

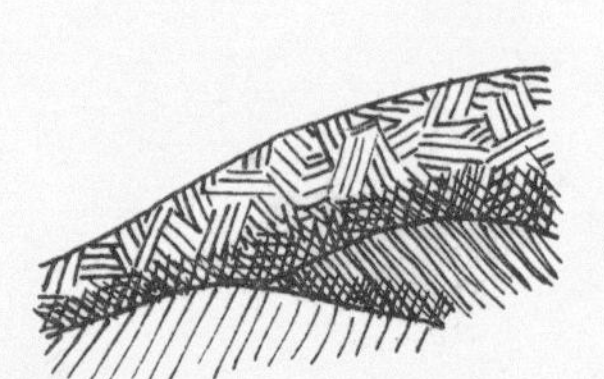

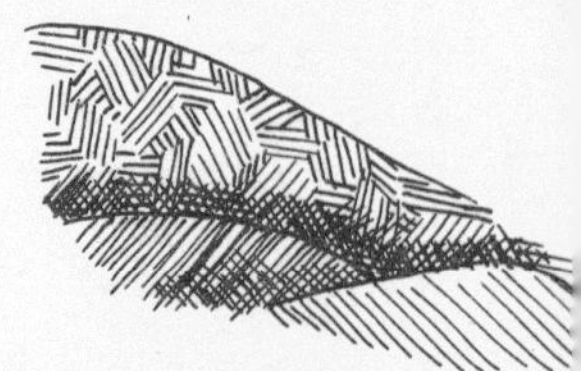

Fly away, Jill.
  (other hand behind back)

Come back, Jack.
  (return one hand)

Come back, Jill.
  (return other hand)

KNOCK, KNOCK
(Fingerplay)

Knock, knock,
(knock on child's forehead)

Peek in,
(open child's eye)

Open the latch,
(push up tip of child's nose)

And walk right in.
(walk fingers into child's mouth)

How do you do Mr. Chin, Chin, Chin?
(wiggle child's chin)

LITTLE GREEN FROG

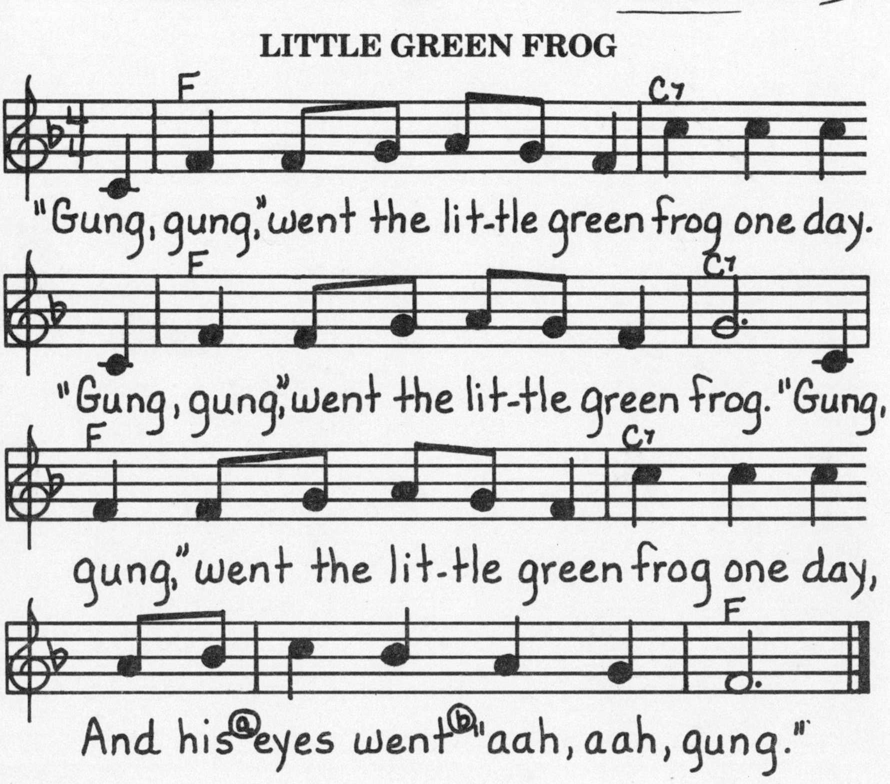

Actions:
a) fingers around eyes b) stick out tongue

JACK AND JILL
(Fingerplay)

Jack and Jill went up the hill,
To fetch a pail of water.
(thumbs straight up, alternating upward)
Jack fell down and broke his crown,
(wiggle one thumb and wrist down)
And Jill came tumbling after.
(wiggle other thumb and wrist down)
Then up got Jack and said to Jill,
(bring one thumb up, then other)
As in his arms he took her,
(cross thumbs)
"Brush off that dirt for you're not hurt,
(brush one thumb with other thumb)
Let's fetch that pail of water."
(continue brushing)
So Jack and Jill went up the hill
To fetch the pail of water,
(thumbs up again)
And took it home to Mother dear,
(bring thumbs slowly down together)
Who thanked her son and daughter.
(thumbs meet)

BUMBLEBEE
(Fingerplay)

Bumblebee was in the barn,
(circle finger in air)
Carrying his dinner under his arm.
(circle finger closer to child)
Bzzzzzzz.....
(gently poke child)

WHERE IS THUMBKIN?
(Tune: Are You Sleeping?)

2. Pointer
3. Tall Man
4. Ring Man
5. Baby
6. All the Men

Suggestion: Use with right hand, left hand, right foot, left foot.

Actions:
a) place hands behind back b) show one thumb, then other c) bend one thumb
d) bend other thumb e) wiggle thumbs away, one at a time

'ROUND THE GARDEN
(Fingerplay)

[a]'Round and 'round the garden,
Goes the little mouse.
[b]Up, up, up he creeps,
Up into his house.

Actions:
a) hold child's hand, palm up, with other hand, circle your index finger around palm b) creep fingers up child's arm, tickling under chin or armpit

HERE IS THE CHURCH
(Fingerplay)

Here is the church,
(fold hands, fingers inside)

And here is the steeple.
(index fingers up)

Open the doors,
(thumbs apart)

And see all the people.
(wiggle inside fingers)

Close the doors,
(thumbs together)

And hear them pray.
(hands to ear)

Open the doors,
(thumbs apart)

And they all walk away.
(fingers walk away)

FIVE LITTLE FISHIES

(Fingerplay)

Five little fishies swimming in a pool,
(wiggle five fingers)

First one said, "The pool is cool."
(one finger up) (wrap arms around body)

Second one said, "The pool is deep."
(two fingers up) (hands measure deep)

Third one said, "I want to sleep."
(three fingers up) (rest head on hands)

Fourth one said, "Let's dive and dip."
(four fingers up) (hand dives and dips)

Fifth one said, "I spy a ship."
(five fingers up) (peer out under hand)

Fisherman's boat comes,
(fingers form V and move away from body)

Line goes ker-splash,
(pantomime throwing fishing line)

Away the five little fishies dash.
(wiggle five fingers away)

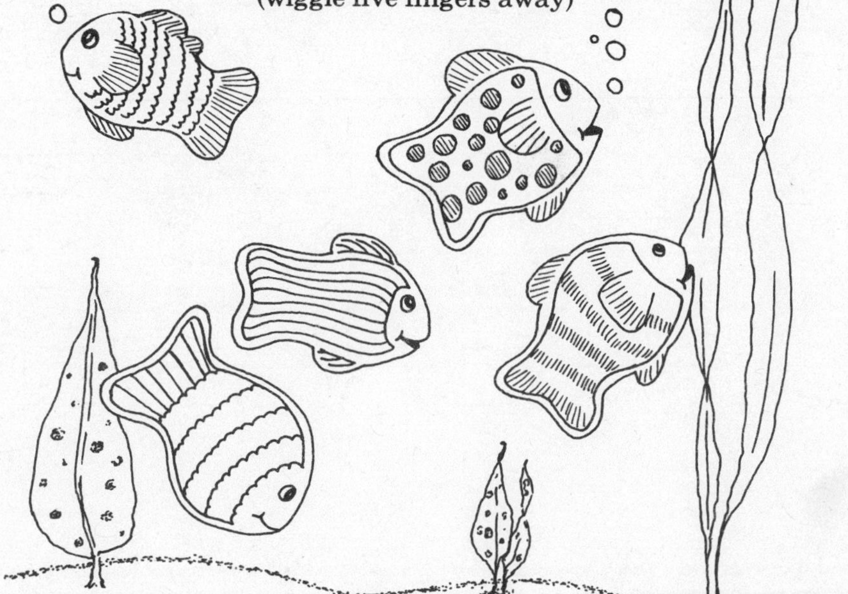

How many more miles did you say?

THIS OLD MAN

2. [a]This old man, [k]he played two,
   [l]He played nick-nack on my shoe;
   With a [d]nick-[e]nack [f]paddy [g]whack,
   [h]give a dog a bone,
   [a]This old man came [i]rolling [j]home.
3. . . .three. . .on my knee (tap knee)
4. . . .four. . .on my door (tap forehead)
5. . . .five. . .on my hive (tap fist)
6. . . .six. . .on my sticks (tap pointer fingers together)
7. . . .seven. . .up in heaven (point to heaven)
8. . . .eight. . .on my gate (tap forearm in front of you)
9. . . .nine. . .on my spine (tap on backbone)
10 . . .ten. . .once again (clap hands)

Actions:
a) hands on hips b) hold up one finger c) pointer finger tap thumb of opposite hand d) slap right thigh with right hand e) slap left thigh with left hand f) slap left shoulder with right hand g) slap right shoulder with left hand h) hands out front, palms up i) roll hands over each other j) thumbs point back over shoulders k) hold up two fingers l) pointer finger tap shoe

2. Do not sing "Rabbit" but do motion.
3. Do not sing "Rabbit" and "fly," but do motions.
4. Do not sing "Rabbit," "fly" and "ear," but do motions.

Actions:
a) hands make rabbit ears b) fingers fly away c) point to ear d) flick ear

THE FINGER BAND

(Tune: Mulberry Bush, p. 41)

1. The Finger Band has come to town,
   Come to town, come to town,
   The Finger Band has come to town,
   So early in the morning.
2. The Finger Band can play the drums...
3. flute
4. clarinet
5. trumpet
6. violin
7. trombone
8. piano
9. guitar
10. The Finger Band has gone away...

Pantomime playing the various instruments.

DOWN BY THE STATION

(Round)

Actions:
a) arms at sides, elbows bent, move hands forward and back in circular motion b) pull imaginary cord

THE TRAIN

S.N. *Susan Nipp*

2. The engineer toots his horn,
   Toot.... (pull imaginary cord in rhythm)
3. The crossing gates come right down,
   Clang... (arms up, elbows bent, hands move down toward each other and back up in rhythm)
4. The people on the train get bumped around,
   Bumpety bump ... (body moves up and down)

Actions:
a) arms at side, elbows bent, move arms forward and back in circular motion

BINGO

2. ...(Clap)-I-N-G-O...
3. ...(X)-(X)-N-G-O...
4. ...(X)-(X)-(X)-G-O...
5. ...(X)-(X)-(X)-(X)-O...
6. ...(X)-(X)-(X)-(X)-(X)...

Suggestion: Substitute child's favorite animal and spell child's name.

* Guitar play in E (E, A, B7)

JOHN JACOB JINGLEHEIMER SCHMIDT

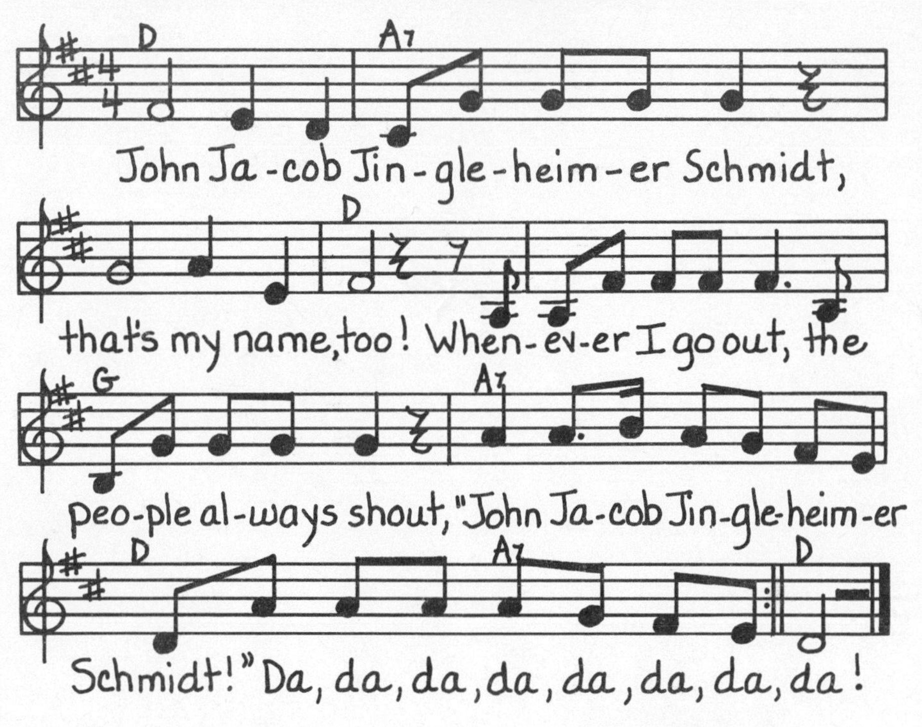

Repeat four times, each time softer, except loudly on the "da da."

Actions:
a) form a peaked roof with finger tips touching b) shade eyes, peer out window
c) middle and forefinger up, make fingers hop d) pantomime knocking e) wave hands
f) knock on head g) beckon rabbit h) rub hands together

* Guitar play in E (E, A, B7)

OLD MACDONALD HAD A FARM

2. And on his farm he had some ducks, E-I-E-I-O.
With a [b] quack, quack here and a quack, quack there,
Here a quack, there a quack, ev'rywhere a quack, quack,
[a]Chick, chick here, and a chick, chick there,
Here a chick, there a chick, ev'rywhere a chick, chick,
Old MacDonald had a farm, E-I-E-I-O.
3. cow - [c] moo, moo (Repeat duck, chick sounds).
4. turkey - [d]gobble, gobble (Repeat cow, duck, chick sounds.)
5. pig - [e]oink, oink (Repeat turkey, cow, etc.)
6. donkey - [f] hee haw (Repeat pig, etc.)

Actions:
a) bob head b) flap elbows c) milk cow d) make turkey tail by hooking thumbs and spreading fingers e) push up tip of nose f) hands up to make ears

Suggestion: Old MacDonald Had a Band - Use instrument names, make their sounds and pretend to play.

Another day, another diaper

Use child's name and sing about what he is wearing.

ONE, TWO, BUCKLE MY SHOE
(Scale Song)

Suggestion: Hold up correct number of fingers.

RICKETY, TICKETY
(Fingerplay)

Rickety, tickety, look at me.
How many fingers do you see?

Example: Hold up two fingers.
If child answers "one" say,
"One you say, but there are two."
Repeat until correct, then praise child.

MY NAME AND ADDRESS
(Tune: Rain, Rain, Go Away, p. 32)

My name is ________________,
child's name
This is my address,
________________,
address
__________, __________.
city state

THE ALPHABET SONG

(Tune: Twinkle, Little Star, p. 33)

A-B-C-D-E-F-G, H-I-J-K-L-M-N-O-P,
Q-R-S, T-U-V, W-X, Y-Z,
Now I know my A-B-Cs,
Tell me what you think of me.

RIGHT HAND, LEFT HAND

(Fingerplay)

This is my right hand,
I'll raise it up high.
(right hand up)

This is my left hand,
I'll touch the sky.
(left hand up)

Right hand,
(show right palm)

Left hand,
(show left palm)

Roll them around.
(roll hands over and over)

Left hand,
(show palm)

Right hand,
(show palm)

Pound, pound, pound.
(pound fists together)

TEN LITTLE FINGERS

(Tune: Ten Little Indians)

2. Ten little, nine little, eight little fingers,
   Seven little, six little, five little fingers,
   Four little, three little, two little fingers,
   One finger on my hand.

Suggestion: Count other things such as toes, rocks, flowers, etc.

DAYS OF THE WEEK

RAIN, RAIN, GO AWAY

Suggestion: Use child's name.

THERE IS THUNDER

(Tune: Are You Sleeping? p. 15)

[a]There is thunder, there is thunder,
Hear it roar, hear it roar,
[b]Pitter, patter, rain drops,
Pitter, patter, rain drops,
[c]I'm all wet! I'm all wet!

Actions:
a) pound floor with palms of hands
b) slap knees alternately and quickly
c) shake rain off hands

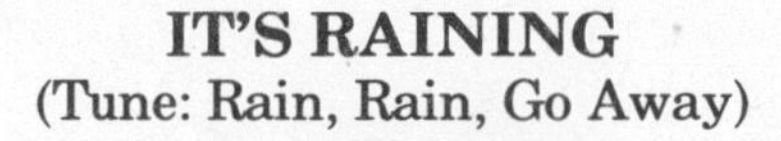

IT'S RAINING

(Tune: Rain, Rain, Go Away)

It's raining, it's pouring,
The old man is snoring.
He went to bed and bumped his head
And couldn't get up in the morning.

TWINKLE, TWINKLE, LITTLE STAR

Jane Taylor 1806

'ROUND THE CLOCK

(Tune: Twinkle, Little Star)

Round the clock the hours go,
  Sometimes fast and sometimes slow,
Tell me what the two hands say,
  They will tell the time of day,
Eight o'clock, it's time for bed.
  Come with me you sleepyhead.

Suggestion: Make up your own rhyme for other times of day.

(Twelve o'clock, it's time to eat,
  Come with me, we'll have a treat.)

Wiggleworm workout
14

LOOBY LOO

2. left hand
   (After each verse, join hands and circle around on chorus.)
3. right foot
4. left foot
5. head
6. whole self

Actions:
a) join hands, circle to left b) stop circling, do as words indicate throughout verse

NOW TALL, NOW SMALL

Actions:
a) squatting position to standing b) back to squatting c) curl into a ball

ANIMAL POEM
(Action Poem)

Pam Beall

I'm a little kitty,
I love to tippy toe.
Won't you do it with me?
Ready now, let's go.

I'm a little rabbit,
I love to hop, hop, hop.
Come on and do it with me.
It's fun; we'll never stop

I'm a great big elephant,
I take big steps so slow.
I'd love to have you join me,
Ready now? Let's go.

I'm a little dog,
I love to run and run.
If you would do it with me,
We could have such fun.

WALKING, WALKING

(Tune: Are You Sleeping? p. 15)

Walking, walking, walking, walking,
  Hop, hop, hop, hop, hop, hop.
Running, running, running,
  Running, running, running,
Now let's stop, now let's stop.

JIMMY CRACK CORN

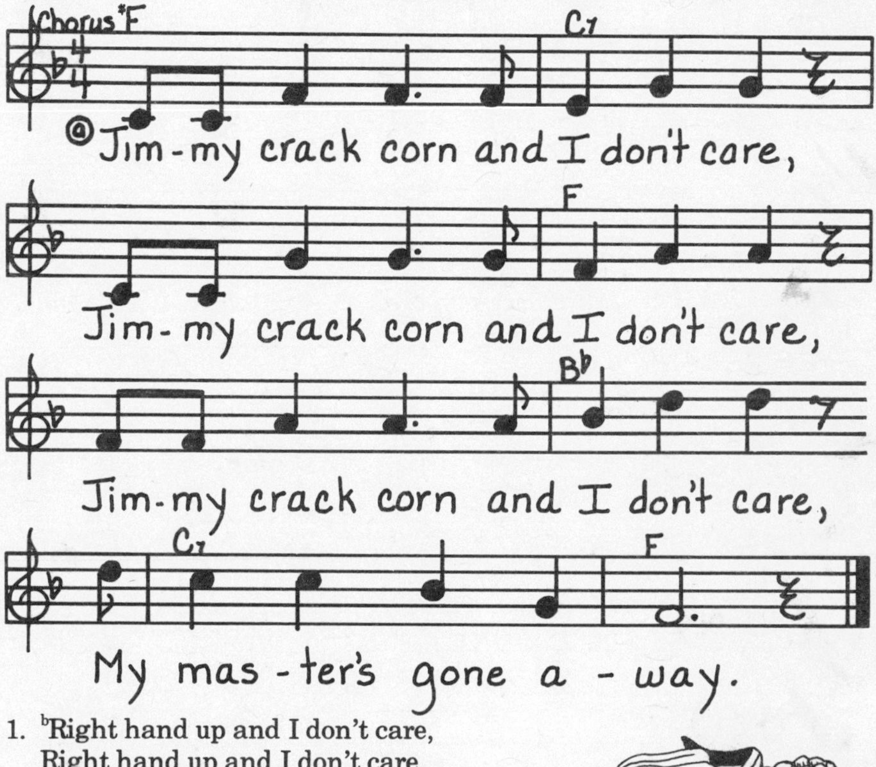

1. [b]Right hand up and I don't care,
   Right hand up and I don't care,
   Right hand up and I don't care,
   [c]My master's gone away.
   (Chorus sung after each verse)
2. [d]Left hand up...
3. [e]Both hands up...

Actions:
a) circle to left throughout chorus b) hold right hand up and walk to center of circle
c) hand down, move back out to form circle d) hold left hand up, walk to center of circle e) both hands up, walk to center of circle

* Guitar play in E (E, A, B7)

BABY BIRD
(Scale Song)

Pam Beall

Actions:
a) on arms and knees, fetal position, head down   b) head pops up   c) tail pops up
d) stand up   e) flap elbows   f) flap arms   g) twirl around and around   h) fall down

RING AROUND THE ROSY

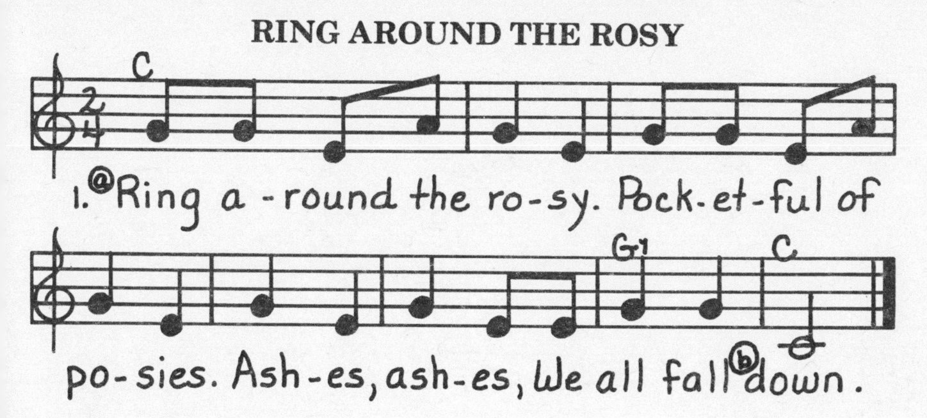

2. Tiptoe 'round the rosy...
3. Skip
4. Hop
5. Run

Actions:
a) join hands, circle to left
b) all fall down

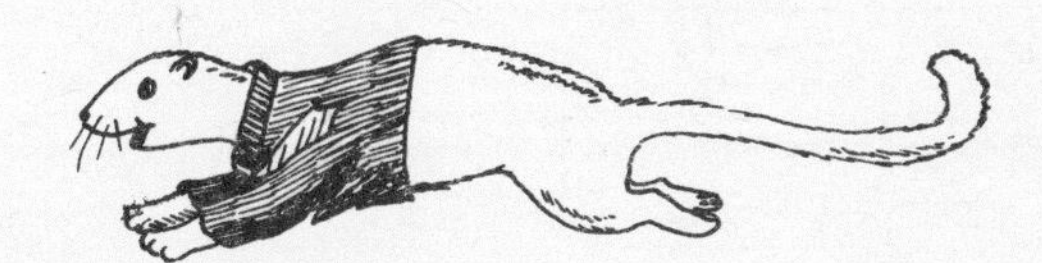

POP! GOES THE WEASEL

Suggestions:
1. Roll hands while singing, clap on POP.
2. Walk in circle, fall on POP.

Actions:
a) make circle in air with finger b) chase one hand with the other hand c) hands at either side of head, rock sideways d) clap

I'M A LITTLE TEAPOT

Actions:
a) act very stout b) place one hand on hip c) extend other arm to side, elbow and wrist bent d) nod head vigorously e) tip sideward in direction of extended arm

I'M A LITTLE SNOWMAN

(Tune: I'm a Little Teapot, p. 40)

I'm a little snowman, short and fat,
Here is my broomstick, here is my hat.
When the sun comes out, I melt away,
Down, down, down, down, whoops...
I'm a puddle! (spoken)

Pantomime words.

THE MULBERRY BUSH

1. This is the way we wash our face
2. Comb our hair
3. Brush our teeth
4. Put on our clothes
5. Etc.

Suggestion: For circle game, join hands and circle around on chorus after each verse. Act out motions on verses.

IF YOU'RE HAPPY

2. . . . stomp your feet (stomp, stomp) . . .
3. . . . shout hurray (Hurray!) . . .
4. . . . do all three (clap, clap, stomp, stomp, hurray!) . . .

* Guitar play in E (E, A, B7)

PETER HAMMERS

(Tune: What Are You Wearing? p. 28)

1. Peter hammers with one hammer, one hammer,
   one hammer, (pound one fist on floor or leg)
   Peter hammers with one hammer all day long.
2. Two hammers (pound two fists)
3. Three hammers (pound two fists, one foot)
4. Four hammers (pound two fists, two feet)
5. Five hammers (pound two fists, two feet, nod head up and down)
6. Peter's very tired now... (rub eyes, then lay head on hands)

REACH FOR THE SKY

THREE BLUE PIGEONS

2. Two blue pigeons sitting on a wall,
   Two blue pigeons sitting on a wall.
   Another flew away! O-o-o-o-o-h. (spoken)

3. One blue pigeon sitting on a wall,
   One blue pigeon sitting on a wall.
   And the third flew away! O-o-o-o-o-h.

4. No blue pigeons sitting on a wall,
   No blue pigeons sitting on a wall.
   One flew back! Whee-ee-ee-ee!

5. One blue pigeon sitting on a wall,
   One blue pigeon sitting on a wall.
   Another flew back! Whee-ee-ee-ee!

6. Two blue pigeons sitting on a wall,
   Two blue pigeons sitting on a wall.
   And the third flew back! Whee-ee-ee-ee!

7. Three blue pigeons sitting on a wall,
   Three blue pigeons sitting on a wall.
   (Clap happily while singing)

Suggestion: Three children sit on a bench. All children sing while the three act out the words.

ONE ELEPHANT WENT OUT TO PLAY

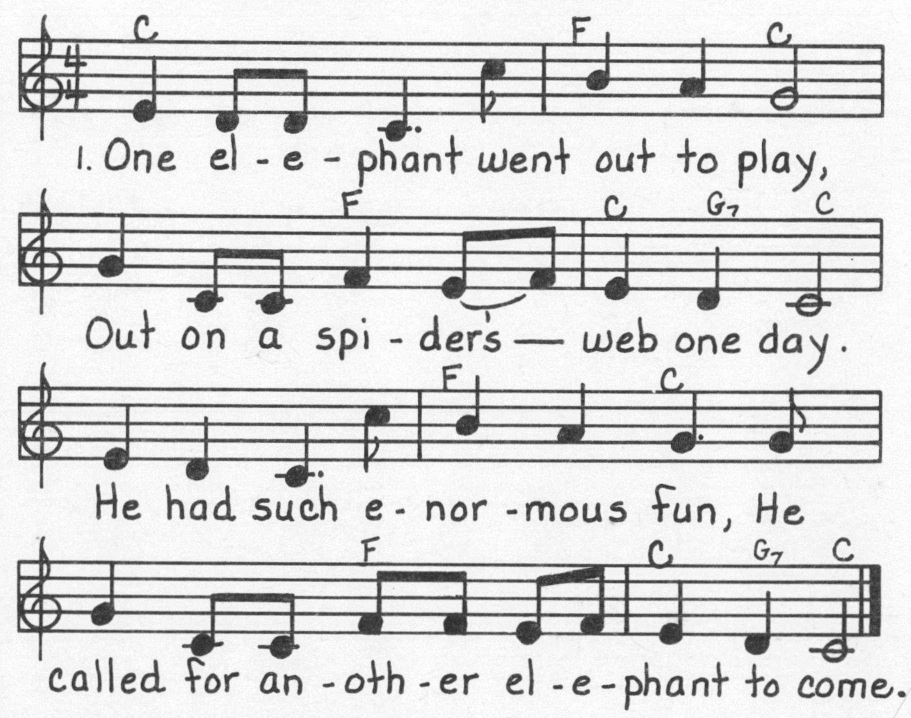

2. Two elephants went out to play…
3. Three elephants went out to play, etc.

Game: One child walks around room like an elephant. At the end of the verse, he chooses another 'elephant' to join behind him. At the end of each verse, the last 'elephant' chosen selects a new 'elephant'. Continue until several children are imitating elephants.

HEAD AND SHOULDERS

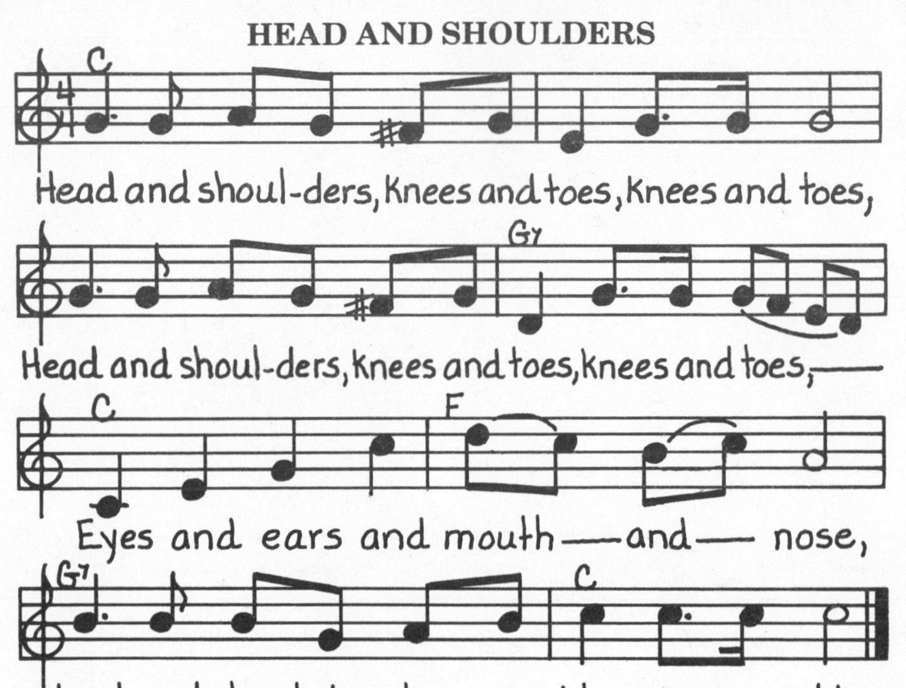

Suggestions: Point to body parts as singing. Repeat, leaving out different body parts each time.

JACK AND JILL

(Scale Song)

Actions:

a) squat down and as notes move up, move body slowly to standing position b) start moving down as notes move down ending in squatting position

THIS IS THE WAY

(Tune: Mulberry Bush, p. 41)

1. This is the way the ladies ride,
   Ladies ride, ladies ride,
   This is the way the ladies ride,
   Tri-tree, tri-tree, tri-tree.
   (bounce child gently on knees)
2. Gentlemen ride — gallop-a-gallop-a-trot!
   (bounce faster)
3. Farmers ride — hobbledy-hobbledy-hoy!
   (bounce harder)

TROT TO BOSTON

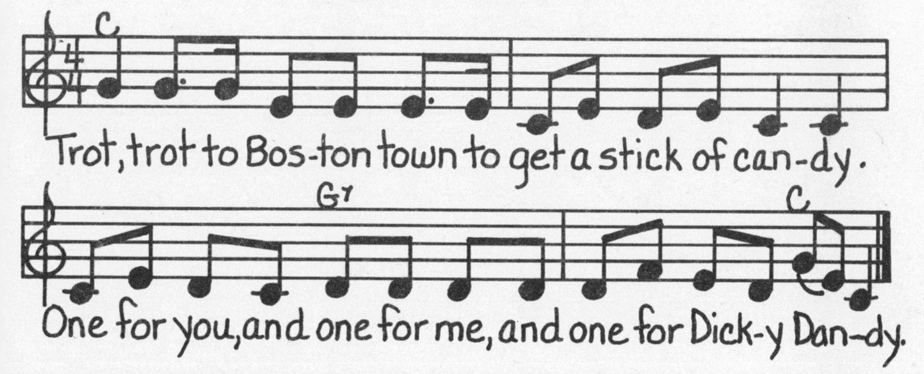

Cross legs, bounce child on foot. Near end of song, gently drop child to floor (surprise).

2. Teddy Bear, Teddy Bear, go upstairs,
   Teddy Bear, Teddy Bear, say your prayers,
   Teddy Bear, Teddy Bear, switch off the light,
   Teddy Bear, Teddy Bear, say good-night.

Pantomime the words.

Whew! It's bedtime.

Suggestion: Substitute child's name for 'baby.'

* Guitar play in E (E, A, B7)

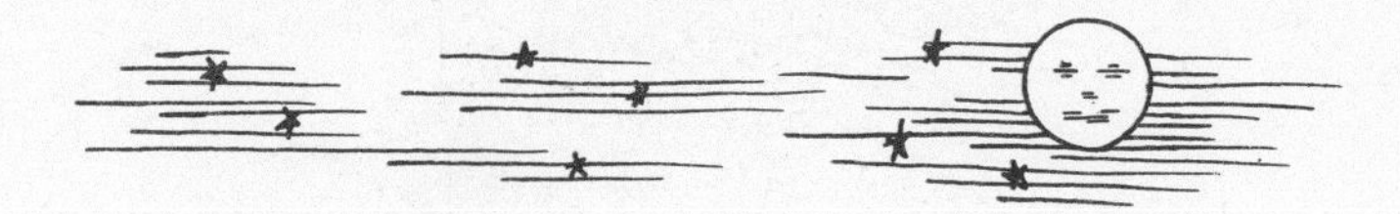

SLEEP, BABY, SLEEP

ALL NIGHT, ALL DAY

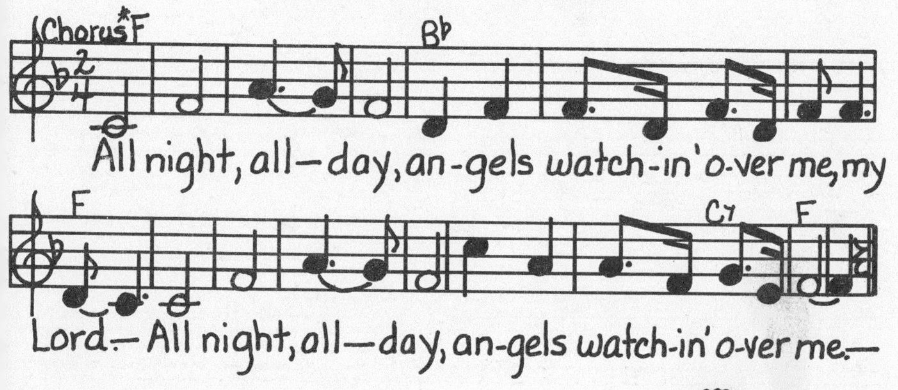

1. When at night I go to sleep,
   Angels watchin' over me, my Lord,
   Pray the Lord my soul to keep,
   Angels watchin' over me.

   (Repeat chorus)

* Guitar play in E (E, A, B7)

ALL THE PRETTY LITTLE HORSES
Dm Gm Am
Hush-a-bye, don't you cry, Go to sleep-y lit-tle
When you wake, you shall have all the pret-ty lit-tle
Dm Am Dm
ba-by. Blacks and bays, dap-ples and grays,
hors-es.
Am Dm
coach and six-a-lit-tle hors-es. Hush-a-bye,
Gm Am Dm
don't you cry, Go to sleep-y lit-tle ba-by.

HUSH, LITTLE BABY

2. If that mockingbird don't sing,
   Papa's gonna buy you a diamond ring.
3. If that diamond ring turns brass,
   Papa's gonna buy you a looking glass.
4. If that looking glass gets broke,
   Papa's gonna buy you a billy goat.
5. If that billy goat don't pull,
   Papa's gonna buy you a cart and bull.
6. If that cart and bull turn over,
   Papa's gonna buy you a dog named Rover.
7. If that dog named Rover don't bark,
   Papa's gonna buy you a horse and cart.
8. If that horse and cart fall down,
   You'll still be the sweetest little baby in town.

Another holiday...so soon?
Be Mine

JACK-O-LANTERN
(Fingerplay)

Sometimes big and sometimes small,
(arms form large circle, then small)

But always round and yellow,
(draw circle in air)

When children make my famous grin,
(grin, showing teeth)

Then I'm a scary fellow.
(make scary face)

CHICKAMY, CHICKAMY, CRANEY CROW

Game: Choose a child to be the witch. The witch hides her eyes and turns her back while a group of children sing in a teasing way near her. At the count of twelve, the witch comes out of hiding and tries to catch as many children as she can. Children are 'safe' if they reach a predetermined point.

TEN LITTLE WITCHES

(Tune: Ten Little Indians, p. 31)

1. One little, two little, three little witches,
   Four little, five little, six little witches,
   Seven little, eight little, nine little witches,
   Ten witches in the sky.
2. Ten little, nine little, eight little witches,
   Seven little, six little, five little witches,
   Four little, three little, two little witches,
   One little witch, "Bye, bye!"

GOBBLE, GOBBLE

(Fingerplay)

[a]A turkey is a funny bird,
[b]His head goes wobble, wobble,
And he knows [c]just one word,
[d]Gobble, gobble, gobble.

Actions:
a) make turkey tail by hooking thumbs and spreading fingers b) shake from side to side c) hold up one finger d) shake head, sound like turkey

OVER THE RIVER

2. Over the river and through the woods,
   Trot fast my dapple gray.
   Spring over the ground like a hunting hound
   For this is Thanksgiving Day.
   Over the river and through the woods,
   Now Grandmother's face I spy.
   Hurrah for the fun, is the pudding done?
   Hurrah for the pumpkin pie.

CHRISTMAS IS COMING

S. Nesbitt 1600's

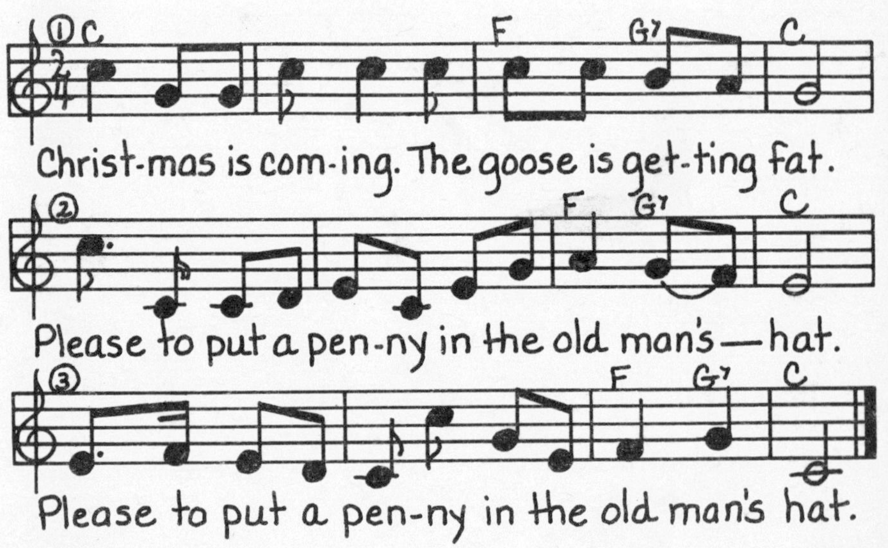

Suggestion: Can be sung as a round

THE CHIMNEY
(Fingerplay)

Here is the chimney,
(make fist with thumb inside)

Here is the top,
(other hand over fist)

Open the lid,
(remove hand)

Out Santa will pop!
(pop up thumb)

WE WISH YOU A MERRY CHRISTMAS

Chorus G C A7 D7 G C D7 G

[a]We wish you a Mer-ry Christ-mas, We wish you a Mer-ry Christ-mas, We wish you a Mer-ry Christ-mas and a Hap-py New Year!

1. [b]Let's all do a little clapping,
   Let's all do a little clapping,
   Let's all do a little clapping,
   And spread Christmas cheer.
   (Chorus sung after each verse)

2. [c]Jumping
3. [d]Twirling

Suggestion: Add your own verses.

Actions:
a) join hands, circle to left, continuing throughout chorus b) clap hands c) jump in place d) twirl in place

SKIDAMARINK

Actions:
a) right elbow in left hand, wiggle fingers b) left elbow in right hand, wiggle fingers c) point to self d) hug self e) point to other person f) arms form circle above head, lean left g) keep circle above head, stand straight h) keep circle above head, lean right i) sweep arms down and form new circle above head

INDEX

All Night, All Day 51
All the Pretty Little Horses 52
Alphabet Song, The 30
Animal Poem* 36
Baby Bird 38
Bingo 23
Bumblebee* 15
Chickamy, Chickamy, Craney Crow 55
Chimney, The* 59
Christmas is Coming 58
Clap Your Hands* 10
Days of the Week 31
Down by the Station 21
Eentsy Weentsy Spider 8
Finger Band, The 21
Five Little Fishies* 17
Gobble, Gobble* 56
Good Morning 28
Good Night 50
Grandma's Glasses* 10
Head and Shoulders 46
Here is the Beehive* 9
Here is the Church* 16
Hickory, Dickory Dock 11
Hush, Little Baby 53
If You're Happy 42
I'm a Little Snowman 41
I'm a Little Teapot 40
It's Raining 32
Jack and Jill* 14
Jack and Jill 46
Jack-O-Lantern* 55
Jimmy Crack Corn 37
John Jacob Jingleheimer Schmidt 24
Knock, Knock* 13
Little Cabin in the Wood 25

*Titles with asterisks are fingerplays, which are rhymes illustrated by the use of finger motions.

Little Green Frog 13
Little Peter Rabbit 20
Looby Loo 35
Mother's Knives and Forks* 9
Mulberry Bush, The 41
My Name and Address 29
Now Tall, Now Small 36
Old MacDonald Had a Farm 26
One Elephant Went Out to Play 45
One, Two, Buckle My Shoe 29
Over the River 57
Peter Hammers 43
Pop! Goes the Weasel 39
Rain, Rain, Go Away 32
Reach for the Sky 43
Rickety, Tickety* 29
Right Hand, Left Hand* 30
Ring Around the Rosy 39
'Round the Clock 33
'Round the Garden 16
Sleep, Baby, Sleep 51
Skidamarink 60
Teddy Bear 48
Ten Little Fingers 31
Ten Little Witches 56
There is Thunder* 32
This is the Way 47
This Old Man 19
Three Blue Pigeons 44
Three Little Monkeys* 12
Train, The 22
Trot to Boston 47
Twinkle, Twinkle Little Star 33
Two Little Blackbirds* 12
Walking, Walking 37
We Wish You a Merry Christmas 59
What Are You Wearing? 28
Where is Thumbkin? 15

Wee Sing®

by Pamela Conn Beall and Susan Hagen Nipp

Discover all the books and cassettes
in the best-selling WEE SING series!